D0392055

Say It with Music

A Story about Irving Berlin

by Tom Streissguth
illustrations by Jennifer Hagerman

A Carolrhoda Creative Minds Book

Carolrhoda Books, Inc./Minneapolis

To Lou Lou, piano pounder

Copyright © 1994 by Carolrhoda Books, Inc.
All rights reserved. No part of this book may be reproduced,
stored in a retrieval system, or transmitted in any form or by any
means, electronic, mechanical, photocopying, recording, or otherwise,
without the prior written permission of Carolrhoda Books, Inc.,
except for the inclusion of brief quotations in an acknowledged review.

Carolrhoda Books, Inc. ℅ The Lerner Group
241 First Avenue North, Minneapolis, MN 55401

Library of Congress Cataloging-in-Publication Data

Streissguth, Thomas, 1958—
    Say it with music : a story about Irving Berlin / by Tom Streissguth ;
illustrations by Jennifer Hagerman.
        p. cm. — (A Carolrhoda creative minds book)
    Includes bibliographical references.
    Summary: Describes the life of the famous composer of popular
musicals and songs, including "God Bless America."
    ISBN 0-87614-810-0
    1. Berlin, Irving, 1888-1989—Juvenile literature. 2. Composers—
United States—Biography—Juvenile literature.
[1. Berlin, Irving, 1888-1989. 2. Composers. 3. Jews—Biography]
I. Hagerman, Jennifer, ill. II. Title. III. Series.
ML3930.B446S8   1994
782.1'4'092—dc20
[B]   93-4376
                                                                                  CIP
                                                                               AC MN

Manufactured in the United States of America

1 2 3 4 5 6 – I/MA – 99 98 97 96 95 94

Table of Contents

① Passage to New York

It was a cold evening during a long Russian winter. The muddy streets of Moghilev were quiet, and the small wooden homes were dark. Moses Baline, his wife, Lena, and his six children were sleeping. At first, they didn't hear the horsemen who were riding through the streets of the town with sabers, pistols, and torches.

The Balines and other Jewish families lived in a part of Russia called the Pale of Settlement. For centuries, the Russian government had prevented Jews from owning land. In the 1800s, Jews were not allowed to live outside of the Pale. But in Moghilev, Jews could worship freely, and many supported themselves as merchants in the towns. This arrangement didn't stop the terrible pogroms, when horsemen swept through the streets, attacked passersby, scattered livestock, and set fire to the houses.

The men arrived at the home of the Balines. The

family, awakened by the pounding of hooves and the shouts of their neighbors, ran out of their house and into the street. They had no weapons to fight with, and no place to hide. Lena Baline set her children down on a blanket on the hard, frozen ground. Moses and his family watched helplessly as their home burned to ashes.

The Balines had nowhere else to live. Moses was a cantor—a singer who performed during services in the Jewish synagogue. Cantors were poor, and Moses didn't have enough money to buy or build another house. But he did have a cousin who lived in New York City, in the United States. There the Balines could start again.

After many months, Moses had collected enough money to buy a passage for his family on a steamship, the SS *Rhynland*. In September 1893, after weeks of traveling, they finally arrived in the busy harbor of New York. Tugboats maneuvered their ship through the harbor's choppy, gray waters. From the decks, the passengers could see the towering skyscrapers of Manhattan. In front of the ship, a brick building and four towers rose from Ellis Island.

All immigrants to the United States had to pass through the big and noisy halls of Ellis Island.

German, Russian, Italian, and Irish families descended from the *Rhynland* and joined crowds of people waiting in long, slow lines. Men in uniforms inspected them carefully and filled out their immigration papers. Officials sent new arrivals who had diseases such as yellow fever, malaria, or influenza right back to their homelands.

Standing among the waiting passengers were Moses and Lena Baline and their six children—Sarah, Sifre, Benjamin, Rebecca, Chasse, and the youngest, five-year-old Israel. The family had packed everything they owned into eight pieces of luggage. Although they were poor, the Balines were healthy. They passed their inspection, left the immigration building, and boarded a ferry for the island of Manhattan. They would never return to Russia.

Moses's cousin was waiting at the ferry dock. He had found a basement apartment for the Balines on New York's Lower East Side. The Balines later moved to an apartment on Cherry Street, where Moses and Lena and the six children lived in three small rooms on the third floor. To help pay the rent, they took in a lodger.

The Lower East Side was a poor and noisy neigh-borhood crowded by thousands of immigrant families from Europe. Narrow brick tenements, their windows open for air, formed a high wall along the streets. There were no parks, no trees, and no playgrounds. Children fought and played in a stream of traffic. Newsboys sold their papers on the crowded corners. Vendors offered their fruits and vegetables from carts lining the sidewalks. The smells of home cooking and rotting garbage filled the alleys, streets, and apartment halls.

The Balines struggled to survive in this new world. There was no demand for cantors, so Moses took jobs as a poultry inspector and as a housepainter. His son Benjamin worked long hours making shirts, and his daughters rolled cigars in a factory. After school Israel Baline sold newspapers on the streets.

Israel was small and frail, but he learned English quickly and worked hard to earn money for the family. He stood for hours in the late afternoon, calling out the headlines for his customers. To pass the time, he liked to sing to the passing crowds. He learned new songs every day. He could sing German, Italian, and Irish songs by heart. In appreciation, some passersby would throw an extra coin at his feet.

Israel enjoyed singing much more than selling, and his music was earning him as much money as his newspapers. Perhaps one day he would make a better living from his voice.

Every day Israel brought the few pennies he had earned home to his mother. But the Balines were still struggling. Worse, Moses came down with bronchitis from the dust he breathed while painting. In early 1901, his condition grew worse. In the middle of the summer, he died.

Lena, a poor widow who spoke little English, could not support her big family. Soon after the death of his father, Israel left home to make his own way in the world. He had already left school. Now he was fourteen years old, with no job, no money, and no place to live.

Vaudeville

Not far from Cherry Street was the Bowery, a long and wide avenue with laundries, boarding-houses, pawnshops, and bars. Many of the saloons looked the same. Customers entered through a set of small, swinging doors. Simple tables and chairs were set out on a bare, unswept wooden floor. Against one wall was a long bar, where customers spent their idle hours drinking from bottles and beer mugs. Most saloons had an upright piano in the back with a small open space nearby for dancing.

In some establishments, singers and piano players performed late into the night. If the saloon couldn't afford to hire musicians, entertainment was provided by "buskers" who came through the front doors, directly from the streets.

Israel Baline had left home and now lived in a

Bowery boardinghouse, where he paid a few cents a night for a narrow bed and a dirty blanket. He could no longer survive by selling newspapers. But he had a talent for singing and for entertaining people. He had made extra money from singing on the corner. Why not try to make a little more in the saloons?

Every busker needed a catchy name, so he became "Izzy," a name his friends on Cherry Street had given him. He went from bar to bar, singing for the customers. He had several favorite songs. One of them was "Give My Regards to Broadway," a big hit written by a star named George M. Cohan:

Give my regards to Broadway
Remember me to Herald Square
Tell all the boys on Forty-second Street
That I will soon be there!

If the crowd enjoyed his song, they would toss him a nickel or a dime. If he collected fifteen cents, he could afford to pay for a bed that night.

Izzy had no trouble collecting enough to buy food and pay for his bed. As the nickels and dimes flew at his feet, he made up his mind. He was determined to make his future, somehow, in music.

He sang in all the saloons on the Bowery, and soon most of the waiters, bartenders, and customers knew him by name. He could remember the tunes and the lyrics to all the hit songs, like "Mansion of Aching Hearts" and "I Want a Girl Just Like the Girl Who Married Dear Old Dad," two songs by the renowned Harry Von Tilzer.

Izzy sang comic songs, ballads, and patriotic anthems in a strong tenor voice. If a customer requested it, he could even make up new lyrics to any song on the spot. He was making enough money to survive, but Izzy wanted to leave the Bowery bars and break into real show business.

In 1902, a chance came his way. Izzy was hired to sing in the chorus of a traveling musical called *The Show Girl.* But soon after the company reached the town of Binghamton, New York, Izzy was fired. The show wasn't doing well, and the producers decided they didn't need him.

Out of work again, Izzy returned to New York. But during that brief time on the road, he had made up his mind. He wasn't going back to the Bowery, and he wasn't busking in any more saloons. He would ask for steady and respectable work at the offices of Harry Von Tilzer, music publisher.

Popular songs had been printed on loose sheets since the mid-1800s, when families began buying pieces for their own entertainment. Von Tilzer worked far from the Bowery, in a busy suite uptown. His business was songs, which he accepted from local songwriters and then sold as printed sheet music. The customers paid a few pennies for the sheet music, then played and sang the music around the pianos in their living rooms. For every piece of sheet music that sold for five cents, Von Tilzer paid the composer a "royalty" of one cent.

A little bit nervous, Izzy Baline dressed in his best clothes and walked uptown to Von Tilzer's office on Twenty-eighth Street. After a long wait, he was shown in to see the boss.

Von Tilzer didn't have much time for small talk. He glanced at the short, black-haired intruder and immediately asked for a song. Izzy took a breath and began to sing.

"Give my regards to Broadway!
Remember me to Herald Square!"

Von Tilzer listened intently for a few seconds, sat up in his chair and raised his hand for silence. Izzy was hired.

17

He would be a "plugger" for Von Tilzer's songs. The pay was five dollars a week. All he had to do was show up at a nearby theater and take a seat in the balcony. He would wait for the last act—the Three Keatons. When the Three Keatons finished their song, Izzy would stand up and applaud. Then he would repeat the song. He would sing it strong and loud, so the audience would never forget it.

"Okay, here's the place." Von Tilzer shoved a small playbill across his desk. It was an advertisement for a vaudeville show. On the playbill was the name of the show, the cast, curtain time, and the address of the theater: Tony Pastor's Music Hall. This was a famous theater where acts of all kinds—acrobats, musicians, jugglers, dancers, and singers—appeared in variety shows.

Izzy's first night as a plugger was a great success. The Three Keatons—Ma, Pa, and little Buster—told jokes, did some juggling, and finally came to their song. As soon as Izzy stood up to sing, the spotlight swung back from the stage to shine on him. And much to his surprise, the audience didn't seem to mind his performance. Many of them were used to song pluggers. The entire audience soon began to sing along.

After the show, they went home humming the tune to themselves. They couldn't get it out of their heads! The next day, many of them went out to buy the sheet music—which was published by Harry Von Tilzer.

For a few weeks, Izzy made enough money to live. But when the Keatons left town, he was again out of work. Von Tilzer didn't need him anymore.

He was still poor, but Izzy knew he could sing. He soon landed a regular job at the Pelham Cafe, in Chinatown. From eight in the evening until six in the morning, he served food, liquor, and music. The Pelham was a step up from the Bowery. Mike Salter, the owner, even had his own piano player, Nick Nicholson.

Many of the customers in the Pelham Cafe were wealthy people from uptown or from overseas. Late at night—after the uptown restaurants and theaters had closed—they liked to visit Chinatown's less respectable places.

Izzy's singing was a big hit with the customers. He had an amazing memory for song lyrics and melodies, and a knack for making up silly lyrics. He loved performing for an audience, and he especially loved the extra coins that were dropping onto his serving tray. Mike Salter saw that his singing waiter was becoming the cafe's main attraction.

Salter was a smart businessman. He would do almost anything to get more customers in the door. But competition among Chinatown restaurants was tough. A place like the Pelham Cafe could go out of style—and out of business—in a hurry. So when Mike heard that the pianist at another bar had made up a song and published it, he decided that the Pelham Cafe had to have one of its own.

For their boss and for the Pelham Cafe, Izzy and Nick Nicholson volunteered to make up a song. Izzy wrote down some lyrics. Nick banged out a tune on his upright piano. Their piece was a sentimental ballad called ''Marie from Sunny Italy'':

Oh, Marie, 'neath the window I'm waiting.
Oh, Marie, please don't be so aggravating.
Meet me while the summer moon is beaming.
For you and me the little stars are gleaming.
Please come out tonight, my queen,
Can't you hear my mandolin?

Izzy and Nick wrote their tune down and brought it to the office of Joseph Stern, music publisher.

Mr. Stern agreed to print the sheet music. But instead of royalties, he paid the songwriters a one-time fee of seventy-five cents. Izzy and Nick agreed to split their profit. Because he was the singer, Izzy accepted thirty-seven cents for his lyrics, while Nick earned thirty-eight.

Izzy had published his first song. There was only one catch—Stern wanted a different name to print on the sheet music. A name like Israel Baline sounded much too serious and might hurt sales. So Izzy came up with a new name for himself: Irving Berlin.

Ragtime

Irving was now singing and waiting tables at Jimmy Kelly's restaurant, on Union Square near Tony Pastor's Music Hall. After their final act, Tony Pastor's vaudeville stars liked to walk over to Jimmy Kelly's. Many of them showed up just to hear the hilarious singing waiter. Berlin was happy to oblige his listeners with any request, be it fast or slow, happy or sad.

One of his favorite numbers was a parody of a song called "Are Ye Coming Out Tonight" by a songwriter named Max Winslow. Word soon got back to Winslow that a waiter at Jimmy Kelly's was having fun with one of his tunes. Winslow went down to the restaurant to hear for himself. He could see right away that Berlin was a natural performer. The customers were straining to hear the comic lyrics and banging their tables in time to the music.

Winslow and Berlin became fast friends. They rented an apartment together, and Berlin was soon meeting musicians, singers, and theater producers. Winslow had made many friends in the music world through Ted Snyder, his boss at the music publishing firm of Waterson & Snyder. Winslow also introduced Irving to a composer named Edgar Leslie.

After they met, Leslie and Berlin began writing music together. Their first song was called "Wait, Wait, Wait." They sold the tune to Harry Von Tilzer, the publisher who had paid Irving five dollars a week to plug songs in a music hall. This time, Berlin made out a little better—his share of the royalties was two hundred dollars.

Von Tilzer was happy to pay it. A hit song that sold well in music stores, department stores, and drugstores could bring its author and its publisher thousands of dollars every week. In his very first year in business, Von Tilzer had sold five million copies of sheet music. Famous singers like Al Jolson and Eddie Cantor were now performing his songs in vaudeville theaters, while Von Tilzer's pluggers worked on street corners, in saloons, at ballparks—any public place that was likely to have a crowd of future customers.

Selling a hit song was easy, but writing that song could be terribly hard. Even the most famous songwriters had hundreds of failures—songs that didn't even sell enough to cover the cost of printing. The competition in the business was fierce, and in order to make money publishers had to try to reach the widest possible audience.

So songwriters kept to a simple formula, hoping that something in their words or melodies would catch on with the public. All their songs had a verse—which could be as short as eight bars, or much longer—and a chorus of eight or sixteen bars. The verses carried the "action" of the song, and the chorus was repeated after each verse. Usually, the chorus repeated the song's title.

Although he couldn't read music, and had no training as a pianist or as a composer, Berlin was a genius at making up these simple songs. A common phrase or idea would come into his head. He used the phrase as a title and wrote a set of lyrics around it. At the same time, he worked out a melody at the piano. The notes were carefully repeated, over and over, and changed until they sounded just right. An assistant worked by his side to write down the music.

Most popular songs were about love, and Berlin's

were no exception. But his favorite kind of song was the dialect song, which used street slang or the accents of a foreign language such as Italian. One day a vaudeville singer from Tony Pastor's came to Irving with a request. The singer would pay ten dollars for a dialect song about the famous Italian marathon runner Dorando Pietri.

In the Olympic Games of 1908, Dorando had arrived first in the stadium after running the marathon, a footrace of more than 26 miles. But just before he crossed the finish line, a group of cheering fans surrounded him. The Olympic judges ruled that he had received help from the crowd, and Dorando was disqualified.

Berlin gladly accepted the offer. He made up a set of lyrics in Italian dialect. The song described a barber who bets all his money on Dorando and loses. The story was sad, but it was also funny. When Irving presented the "Dorando" lyrics to his client, however, the singer replied that he had changed his mind and was no longer interested.

Berlin took his song to the offices of Waterson & Snyder. Mr. Waterson agreed to hear the words. After Irving recited "Dorando," Waterson asked if there was any music for the tune.

"Of course," said Irving.

"All right, I'll pay you twenty-five dollars for it. Just dictate your tune to the arranger." Waterson directed Irving to a small office. Inside were a man, a piano, and a pile of blank sheet music.

In fact, there was no music to "Dorando." Irving didn't know what to do next. He had no idea how he was going to make up music on the spot. But he wasn't going to walk out without selling his song.

He went into the arranger's office, closed the door, and began humming a tune off the top of his head. The arranger, who spent his days writing down all kinds of strange melodies, simply nodded his head without asking any questions. He did his best to render Irving's nervous humming onto the page. Irving thanked the assistant and left quickly.

At Tony Pastor's and in other New York music halls, "Dorando" was a hit. Irving wrote another song for Waterson & Snyder called "Sadie Salome—Go Home." This one didn't make much money. But the name "Irving Berlin" was catching on in New York. And what a way to make a living—making up words to songs!

It was a clear summer day in New York. Irving Berlin sat in a barbershop with his friend George

27

Whiting. After their haircuts were done, the two men strolled outside. "What's on tonight, Izzy?" asked Whiting.

"Nothing much," said Berlin.

"I've got an idea," said Whiting. "Let's go to a show." He added, "I'm free—my wife's gone to the country."

"Hooray!"

Berlin stopped in his tracks and turned to his friend. "We've got ourselves a song!"

One phrase was all he needed. That night, the two stayed home and made up a story in song. It was about a husband who suddenly discovers that "My Wife's Gone to the Country—Hooray!" Ted Snyder wrote a tune, and the sheet music sold 300,000 copies in the music stores. The *New York Journal* asked Berlin to make up a hundred new verses to the song.

Soon Berlin was working for Waterson & Snyder. He was in demand for vaudeville and for the bigger shows on Broadway. In 1910, the Shubert brothers, famous Broadway producers, hired him to write a few songs for their show *Up and Down Broadway*. With the help of Ted Snyder, Berlin wrote "That Beautiful Rag." This was his first "ragtime" song.

Irving Berlin wasn't the first musician to write ragtime. Black musicians in New Orleans and Chicago had been playing it since the 1890s. Ragtime tunes were syncopated, meaning the melodies accented beats that were usually unaccented in other types of music. The music was written in a driving rhythm over a strong and steady bass line.

But ragtime was dance music, and music publishers and songwriters considered it vulgar. Berlin wanted to make it acceptable to theater audiences. The ragtime songs Berlin wrote for *Up and Down Broadway* were the first ever heard on the stage.

"That Beautiful Rag" gave Irving the idea for more ragtime songs. He wrote a short syncopated tune for Jack Alexander, a famous bandleader, and called it "Alexander and His Clarinet." Later he had the song arranged for jazz band and changed its name to "Alexander's Ragtime Band."

Even though it didn't have a lyric, Berlin liked the tune. But there was no demand for songs without words. What were singers supposed to do with instrumentals? "Alexander's Ragtime Band" stayed on the shelf, until a producer named Jesse Lasky bought it for the band at his new restaurant. When he found that his customers were paying no attention to it—no words!—Lasky dropped it.

In the next year, Irving was invited to a dinner in his honor at the Friars Club. The club members, many of whom were big Broadway stars, wanted him to write a song for their private show, the 1911 *Friars Frolic*. Berlin pulled out "Alexander's Ragtime Band" and wrote some lyrics. After they heard the song, the Friars gave a rousing cheer.

The tune began to catch on. Berlin offered it to singers and musicians passing through his office. The more it was heard on the stage, the more it would sell. The jumpy, syncopated melody delighted performers and audiences. Dancers all over the country were bouncing to "Alexander's Ragtime Band." It was played in restaurants and theaters, on the street, and in Tony Pastor's Music Hall. Soon it crossed the Atlantic Ocean and took London and Paris by storm. By the end of 1911, the sheet music had sold two million copies.

In a matter of weeks, "Alexander's Ragtime Band" made Irving Berlin rich and famous. He followed it with another smash hit called "Everybody's Doin' It Now." The newspapers hailed him as the King of Ragtime. The songwriting firm of Waterson & Snyder took on its most popular composer as a partner and changed its name to Waterson, Berlin, and Snyder.

Vaudeville singers could no longer hear Irving perform at Jimmy Kelly's restaurant. Instead of tipping the young singing waiter, they were now fighting for the chance to perform one of his new tunes. One day in 1912, a young performer named Dorothy Goetz showed up at Waterson, Berlin, and Snyder. She marched straight into Irving Berlin's office and announced that she needed a song for her act. Any song of his would do!

Dorothy spotted a small pile of music copy on Berlin's desk. She snatched up the sheets in her hands and began reading them.

"No—it's mine!" said another woman who was barging into the office.

The two grabbed for the music. Loose and torn pages flew around the room. Dorothy pulled her arm back and let go a hard slap. In return, she got a punch in the face. The two singers kicked and screamed. They clawed with their fingers and pulled each other's hair.

After several minutes of this commotion, Irving managed to separate the women. Scratched and disheveled, Dorothy had lost the battle. Her rival walked out of the office with the latest song by Irving Berlin. But Irving found something attractive in Dorothy. He decided to ask her out.

Irving and Dorothy quickly fell in love. They were married a few weeks later in February and decided to spend their honeymoon in Cuba.

American tourists loved the island's tropical breezes and exciting nightlife. But soon after Irving and Dorothy arrived, Dorothy came down with typhoid fever. When the couple returned to New York, Irving called in a team of doctors to care for his wife.

Irving called the doctors over to the apartment every day, but Dorothy didn't recover from the fever. Just five months after the honeymoon, Dorothy died. After the funeral, Irving poured out his sorrow in a sad ballad called "When I Lost You."

Writing the music and lyrics to "When I Lost You" helped Irving to recover from the death of his wife. But he was growing tired of his work and was ready for a change. He didn't enjoy listening to the firm's ten piano players banging out half-finished songs all day long. He didn't need to spend his time listening to amateurs, and he certainly had no trouble writing hit songs on his own. He was sure that he could earn just as much money by taking complete control of the publication of his own music.

By now he had enough money to start up his own

company—Irving Berlin, Inc. He took on Max Winslow as his business partner and moved into new offices uptown, in the heart of the Broadway theater district. Here he could be closer to the shows, and to the show business, where his future lay. He would continue to publish and collect royalties on his vaudeville tunes at Waterson, Berlin, and Snyder. Longer songs that he wrote for Broadway shows were now his property, and his alone.

④

Yip, Yip, Yaphank!

It was 1916. World War I had dragged on for two years in northern Europe. The soldiers of Britain, Germany, and France lived in deep, muddy trenches dug into the ground. From time to time, their generals ordered them to attack across the no-man's-land between the trenches. Artillery shells rained down, planes dropped bombs, and infantry raked the ground with machine gun fire. Hundreds of thousands fell, dead or wounded, while armies gained or lost a few yards of ground.

To Americans it was a bloody, faraway war that nobody would win. Yet the United States supported Britain and France against Germany, and entered the war in 1917. The public wanted to escape from the bad news, and Irving Berlin was happy to provide them with entertainment. He was

36

turning out a new song almost every week, and writing the musical score for a new Broadway show called *Stop! Look! Listen!*

Berlin also wrote patriotic songs that reflected the mood of the times. He was proud of his adopted country and of his own success. He had found a land that made possible the dreams of a poor immigrant. While the war raged in Europe, he made an important decision—he would become a citizen of the United States. There would be no return, ever, to his native land. In 1918, at the age of twenty-nine, he took the formal oath that made him a citizen of the United States.

A few weeks later, he was drafted into the United States Army. Berlin became just another foot soldier, living on the sum of thirty dollars a month at the army's Camp Upton. The base was near the little town of Yaphank, about sixty miles east of New York City on Long Island. Troops gathered at Camp Upton before being shipped across the Atlantic Ocean to France.

Irving Berlin was no longer living like a famous songwriter. He wasn't staying up late with singers, dancers, and producers. Instead he marched for hours in the hot sun and learned how to clean a rifle. He swept the grounds and peeled potatoes in an army kitchen. Worst of all, he went to bed early and awoke to the piercing notes of "Reveille," a simple melody blown on a bugle at the crack of dawn.

Berlin decided quickly that army life didn't suit him. He didn't mind the hundred little tasks he had to perform, or the harsh words of his sergeant. But the army's day began before sunrise, and Berlin liked to sleep past noon. If only he had a proper excuse to ignore that bugle!

He soon had his chance.

The commander of Camp Upton, General Bell, wanted to raise money for a visitors' center at Camp Upton. He called Berlin into his office.

"We want a place where friends and relatives of the men can be made a little more comfortable when they come to visit. It could cost a lot of money— perhaps $35,000—and we thought perhaps you could put on a little show to make that money."

Berlin thought about it. He had met plenty of draftees in the camp who could sing and dance. He could use them to put on a vaudeville show right there. But first he would make a deal.

"Here's the thing, General," Berlin said. "I write at night. Sometimes I work all night when I get an idea. And I couldn't do that if I had to get up in the morning at five, you understand.''

''Why, you don't have to get up at five,'' said the general. ''You just forget about all that. You write this show!''

The general provided a piano and a quiet room, and Berlin got to work. Within a few weeks, he had finished a revue—a collection of songs and funny sketches—that he called *Yip, Yip, Yaphank*.

The revue was a big production. There were marching drills and boxing demonstrations. There were acrobats and jugglers, all in uniform. Soldiers danced in a chorus line, played in comedy sketches, and sang songs—sometimes a little off-key. To give the show some patriotic feeling, Berlin added a song called ''God Bless America.'' But somehow the song didn't seem to fit. Why perform another patriotic tune when so many of them were already being published? The composer dropped ''God Bless America'' from the show at the last minute.

To raise even more money for his visitors' center, General Bell decided to move the show to the Century Theater in New York. This theater had a bigger stage and could hold several thousand spectators.

Opening night was August 19. It was a hot and humid evening, but the theater was sold out. All the big vaudeville stars were there. The audience settled into their seats, and the curtain went up. A lone soldier appeared on the stage.

"Attennnnnn-tion!"

The audience rose to their feet. General Bell appeared at the back of the hall, marched to his box, and took his place.

"At ease!"

The audience sat back down.

Yip, Yip, Yaphank was a smash hit. Berlin himself appeared in every show, sitting alone on stage in front of a tent to sing "Oh, How I Hate to Get Up in the Morning." At the end of the number, he was paraded around the stage on the shoulders of the uniformed actors and singers—to a standing ovation. "Oh, How I Hate to Get Up in the Morning" turned out to be the biggest hit of the show—in fact, the biggest hit of the entire war.

The show ran for thirty-two performances, every one a sellout. After the final number ended on closing night, the band played "We're On Our Way to France." The audience gave the soldiers on stage a rousing ovation. But instead of taking their bows and leaving by the wings, the men marched down into the aisles in formation.

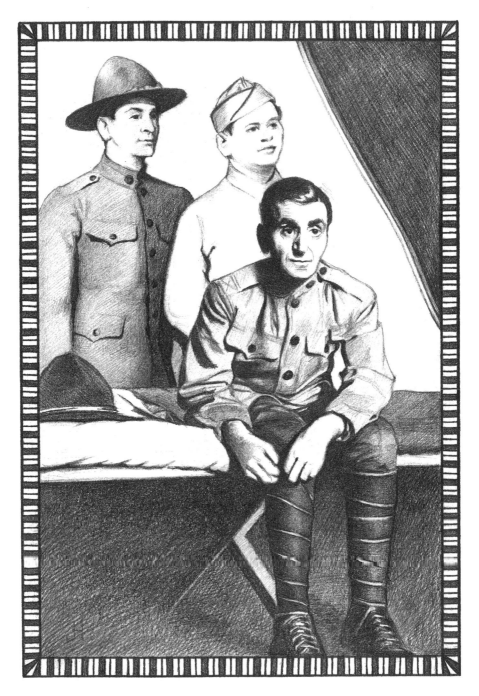

The surprised audience kept their places while the cast of *Yip, Yip, Yaphank* marched to the exits, out into the street, and down to New York harbor. Irving Berlin kept his place on stage. Although he would serve out the rest of the war at Camp Upton, many members of his cast would board a troop ship for Europe that night. Many of them would never return.

⑤

The Music Box

After the war ended in the fall of 1918, millions of army draftees became civilians again. For Irving, it was time to write hit songs and forget about war and soldiering. *Yip, Yip, Yaphank* had made his reputation among Broadway producers. Many of them were now eager to enlist Irving Berlin for their shows.

Berlin was eager to work for them because the music publishing business was going through hard times. Instead of buying sheet music to play on their pianos, customers were buying records for listening. Royalties were still paid to performers and composers, but sales of printed music were falling. Worse, Tin Pan Alley was out of fashion. The ragtime pieces, the comic dialect songs, and the love ballads weren't popular anymore.

The times were changing, and Berlin was determined to change with the times. He no longer wrote funny lyrics or ragtime. His melodies no longer jumped—they flowed across the page and up and down the keyboard. Yet his pieces were still simply constructed, easy to play and remember. They used catchy themes, simple chords, and sweet melodies.

Florenz Ziegfeld, a producer of elaborate musicals, asked Irving to write the music for the *Ziegfeld Follies of 1919*. The show included "A Pretty Girl Is Like a Melody" and "You'd Be Surprised," which sold eight hundred thousand copies and became Irving Berlin's first hit record.

Berlin was having success with nearly every song he wrote. But he had no experience in organizing big productions. When writing for Broadway shows, he always had to rely on a producer. He was little more than a hired hand who put his talents to work for someone else.

Then he met Sam Harris, a successful Broadway

producer who dreamed of building his own theater. It would be only for musicals. He would control the money, the stars, and the shows. He would pay no rent for the use of someone else's theater—all the profits from the shows would belong to him.

But Sam Harris was no musician. He needed a partner who could write the shows, and by his side was one of the most successful composers in the history of Tin Pan Alley. He told Berlin about his idea.

"I've got a name for your theater," Berlin said. "If you want it only for music—how about the Music Box?"

"The Music Box." Harris liked that name. But—"I've got a better name," he said. "Irving Berlin's Music Box!"

"Too much Berlin," Irving replied.

The two men agreed to call it the Music Box. They became partners and bought land on Forty-fifth Street, in the heart of New York's theater district. Old buildings were torn down, and a brand new one went up. The Music Box would feature only the shows of Irving Berlin. The two men spared no expense. The outside of the Music Box was designed to look like a fancy temple. The seats inside were covered in plush velvet. Gold paint was used on the walls and for the wood trim. Workers laid deep carpets on the floor and hung beautiful chandeliers from the ceiling.

The cost rose to more than one million dollars, and Harris and Berlin quickly ran out of money. They turned to Joseph Schenck, a movie producer, to help complete the construction. Schenck agreed to put up some money and become a partner. Finally, the Music Box was ready.

Irving worked around the clock to prepare the dialogue and music for the first *Music Box Revue.* One of his songs was "Say It with Music." It had a beautiful melody, but Berlin had his doubts about it. Somehow it didn't seem to fit the upbeat mood of the show.

The show finally opened on September 22, 1921. It lasted over three hours, and the audience enjoyed every minute of it. The newspaper critics wrote rave reviews. With a full house every night, the *Music Box Revue* made about nine thousand dollars a week, and the partners also earned money from sales of sheet music. "Say It with Music" became a smash hit, selling more than a million records. In a short time, Berlin was able to pay back Joseph Schenck's entire investment.

Berlin wrote three more editions of the *Music Box Revue.* New shows opened in 1922, 1923, and 1924. Money came in from ticket sales and from sheet music. To add a star to the show and make it even more popular, Berlin traveled to Paris to hire an American singer named Grace Moore. Struggling to survive as an opera singer, Moore accepted his offer and joined the *Music Box Revue* in 1923. With her strong, clear voice, she pleased the audiences as well as critics. It seemed Irving Berlin's good luck would never end.

Irving's friends and business partners were living well. They went to parties, danced until morning, and made friends with glamorous movie stars and important politicians. Every new show, every opening night, was a cause for celebration.

But Irving had no taste for this life. He avoided parties and spent most of his nights working at the piano in his apartment. Since the death of his wife in 1912, he had lived and worked alone. If he went out, he would pay a quiet visit to one of his old haunts—the Pelham Cafe in Chinatown, or Jimmy Kelly's. There he felt at home.

One night, in 1924, he brought some friends downtown to Jimmy Kelly's. He walked past the doors of the old saloon where he had once worked as a singing waiter. As usual, many of the customers recognized him. A few people nodded hello. Others turned around in their chairs to catch a glimpse of him. Most of the customers knew better than to approach Irving Berlin. They knew that he liked his privacy.

But as the hour grew late, one young woman gathered up her courage and walked over to his table. She introduced herself as Ellin Mackay. She was tall and good-looking, but also dignified, like an aristocrat. Irving returned her greeting and invited her to sit at his table. They talked for hours.

He had certainly heard of her. Everybody in New York knew about the Mackays, who had struck it rich in a Nevada silver mine. Clarence Mackay, Ellin's father, now owned the highly successful Postal Telegraph Company. With his fortune, Mackay had built a vast estate on Long Island called Harbor Hill. There his family lived in a mansion with fifty rooms and more than one hundred servants. The Mackays had reached the top of New York society.

High society didn't suit Ellin Mackay, however. She liked to come downtown and dance in noisy cabarets. She wrote about these evenings in a new magazine called the *New Yorker*. She was no aristocrat—she wanted to have fun and meet actors, singers, musicians.

After they met at Jimmy Kelly's, Ellin and Irving began going out on the town. They went to shows and movies and walked for hours along the Manhattan streets. Soon there were rumors that they were engaged.

Clarence Mackay had other ideas. He found out about his daughter's friendship with Irving Berlin, and he didn't approve. He didn't like immigrants, musicians, or Jewish people. So he hired private detectives to investigate Berlin. Perhaps they could find out something about Irving that would cool Ellin's interest.

He loved his daughter. But to marry a Jewish songwriter from the Lower East Side? It was as if she was making fun of him. He would soon put an end to it.

Irving began work on the fourth *Music Box Revue* in September 1924, and the show opened in December. He hardly needed to advertise—everyone in New York knew about the Music Box shows.

The newspapers gave the show good reviews. Grace Moore was still drawing her loyal fans. Nevertheless, attendance was poor, and Berlin started to lose money. It seemed that audiences had changed since the end of the war. Lighthearted songs, skits, and dancing were no longer pulling in customers. People wanted something more substantial, more serious.

The future was uncertain for songwriters like Irving Berlin. Movies were providing a new means of entertainment and drawing audiences away from the theater. If people wanted to hear songs, they could stay home and listen to a radio or a record player. No sheet music or pianos were necessary.

The old way of making up a set of easy rhymes, or a funny story, and then setting it to a simple melody, wasn't working. Jazz was the rage in bars and dance halls. Skilled musicians were using marches, popular songs, and ragtime tunes to improvise, or create new melodies on the spot. Jazz was not for amateurs, and many sheet-music publishers, including Waterson, Berlin, and Snyder, were going out of business.

Worse, Berlin was no longer up to the hard task of creating a new show every year. It seemed his life had become nothing more than composing, rehearsing, and worrying about money. He could still write songs, but his inspiration was fading.

The fourth *Music Box Revue* closed after its

shortest run ever—only 186 performances. After the last show, Grace Moore announced that she wanted to return to Europe and perform opera. Berlin could not persuade her to stay. It was the end of the *Music Box Revue.*

Irving realized that his theater would have to stay open somehow. He decided to rent it to other producers. In 1925 a new comic play opened at the Music Box—with neither words nor music by Irving Berlin. It was called *Cradle Snatchers,* and it starred Humphrey Bogart.

Meanwhile, Irving and Ellin were growing closer, despite Clarence Mackay's efforts to keep them apart. One day Mackay phoned Berlin to demand a face-to-face meeting in the offices of the Postal Telegraph Company. As soon as they met, however, the two men immediately began to argue about Ellin. Berlin, who was just as stubborn as Clarence Mackay, quickly left the room.

To help his daughter forget about the composer, Mackay took her on a long trip to Europe. They visited Italy, France, England, and Switzerland and planned to stay abroad for almost a year. But the plan didn't work. Ellin still missed Irving terribly while she was in Europe. Back at home, he was writing a song for her called "Remember."

By the spring of 1925, Berlin was hard at work on another show. Sam Harris had asked him to write the score for a new musical comedy called *The Cocoanuts*. The stars were four brothers who had spent fifteen years in vaudeville: Groucho, Chico, Harpo, and Zeppo. They called themselves the Marx Brothers.

This time Berlin worked on the show with George S. Kaufman, a famous playwright. Kaufman was responsible for the "book," or the dialogue, for the show. But working together on a Broadway musical, even for two skilled professionals, was not easy. The spirit of the words and the style of the music had to match.

Unfortunately, Kaufman and Berlin disagreed about almost everything. Kaufman didn't care for Berlin's music, and Berlin didn't like Kaufman's dialogue. There was one song in particular Kaufman didn't like—"Always." After an argument, Berlin agreed to leave it out of the show. Eventually, Kaufman and Berlin just decided to ignore cach other.

Berlin also became upset when Groucho and his brothers started changing the words to his songs on purpose. They thought they were being funny. But Berlin wanted his songs played and sung just as they were written. There was to be no improvising, no joking around, no "improvements." Irving Berlin, who had started out improvising lyrics as a singing waiter, wouldn't tolerate anyone doing it to his own music.

The Cocoanuts opened in December and had a successful run. The Marx Brothers eventually made a movie of the show. Irving would soon follow them to Hollywood. But his mind was on other things, especially Ellin Mackay. She had been away for almost a year. When she returned, he asked her to marry him.

Early on the morning of January 4, 1926, Irving placed a call to Max Winslow. He asked his old friend to come downtown to City Hall that day and be a witness at his wedding. Around noon, a city clerk pronounced Ellin and Irving to be husband and wife.

Later that day, one of Clarence Mackay's office workers informed his boss of the wedding. The phones at the Postal Telegraph Company were ringing off their hooks. Newspaper reporters wanted to print his reaction to the marriage. He would have to make some kind of a statement. He sat down and wrote that the marriage had been performed without his "knowledge or approval."

After reading his statement to the press, Mackay called his lawyer. He wanted Ellin struck out of his will. She would no longer have any right to her inheritance—ten million dollars.

Ellin Mackay heard of her father's cold reaction and burst into tears. It seemed Clarence Mackay's dislike of Irving Berlin would never cease, not even for the sake of her happiness.

As soon as the news of the wedding came out, reporters began following the newlyweds around town. They were asking questions, demanding statements, and making up stories from rumors and gossip. For Ellin and Irving, there was no escape. It was like acting in a show on a brightly lit stage, with their personal life serving as the music and words.

They would never get free of the mob of reporters, not in New York, not anywhere in the United States. They decided to leave on a honeymoon as soon as possible. Irving called a ticket agency and reserved two places on the steamship *Leviathan,* which would soon be sailing for Europe. He wanted the fanciest room on the ship—the Presidential Suite.

On the morning of January 9, the *Leviathan* weighed anchor and set sail for Southampton,

England. From the deck, Ellin and Irving waved happily to a crowd of well-wishers down on the pier. The ship slowly pulled away from the dock. It was winter, and the wind was cold. But they were finally alone together. Arm in arm, they walked back to the Presidential Suite, where a grand piano was waiting for more inspiration, more music, more songs.

Almost thirty years had gone by since Irving had made his way down the gangplank of the SS *Rhynland* as a poor immigrant. In the years that had passed, he had moved millions of people to laughter and tears with his songs. He had written a hundred hit songs, built his own theater, and won the hand of Ellin Mackay.

The poverty and the pogroms of Russia had driven Israel Baline and his family to this crowded, noisy city. Now Irving Berlin was sailing back to Europe—a happily married man, and a millionaire.

Afterword

After they returned to New York, Irving and Ellin settled into a new apartment, in hopes of leading a quiet life. Their first daughter, Mary Ellin, was born in November 1926. Linda Louise arrived in 1933 and Elizabeth in 1937.

In 1927, Berlin wrote "Blue Skies," which Al Jolson performed in the first feature-length sound movie, *The Jazz Singer*. In 1933 Irving wrote the score for a Broadway show called *As Thousands Cheer*. For the show, he dusted off an old song called "Smile and Show Your Dimple," renaming it "Easter Parade." The show was a success. From the royalties he earned from the song, Irving made a gift to Clarence Mackay, who had lost all his money in the stock market crash of 1929. Eventually, Irving, Ellin, and Clarence stopped arguing.

By the 1930s, Berlin was working in Hollywood. The entire country was facing hard times. The market crash had caused an economic depression.

Audiences needed to forget their troubles at the movies, and Hollywood obliged them with comedies and musicals. Berlin wrote the music for *Top Hat* and *Follow the Fleet,* two movies starring the dance team of Fred Astaire and Ginger Rogers.

Just as the economy improved, another war began brewing in Europe. The United States would again come to the aid of its allies in Europe. Americans were feeling patriotic. Rummaging through his files, Berlin pulled out "God Bless America," the tune he had written originally for *Yip, Yip, Yaphank* and then set aside. He added new words and offered the song to Kate Smith, who had a weekly radio show.

Radio spread Irving Berlin's song across the country and into nearly every home. He had become the most popular composer in the country, and perhaps in the world. After Smith sang "God Bless America" at the New York World's Fair in 1939, it became another Irving Berlin smash hit. It was played on the radio and performed in the movies. Politicians from both parties—Republicans and Democrats—adopted the rousing phrase "God Bless America!" to end their speeches. Many people still believe that the song should replace "The Star-Spangled Banner" as the national anthem.

The song meant a lot to Irving Berlin, who owed his success and fame to his adopted country. He set up a trust fund that would pay all the royalties earned from "God Bless America" to the Boy Scouts and Girl Scouts.

During the war, he also wrote the music for *Holiday Inn,* a film starring Fred Astaire and Bing Crosby. *Holiday Inn* included a song called "White Christmas," sung by Bing Crosby. In the decades that followed, record stores sold more than thirty million copies of "White Christmas." It became the best-selling record of all time.

After the war, Berlin kept working. He wrote scores for the successful Broadway shows *Annie Get Your Gun* in 1946 and *Miss Liberty* in 1949. But as he grew older, popular music kept changing. Simple melodies written for singing gave way to swing music, hectic tunes written for dancing and listening. Swing developed into complex jazz patterns performed by small instrumental groups. In the 1950s came an explosion of rock and roll. By the 1960s, rock had taken over the music world. The music of Irving Berlin was out of style.

In 1962 Berlin wrote the music for a show called *Mr. President.* He hoped the show would bring back some of the magic of the early stage musicals.

He engaged Hollywood stars to play the leading roles and hoped for a successful run—perhaps several years. President John Kennedy and his wife were invited to the opening-night performance at the National Theater in Washington, D.C. But the president showed up late and stayed for only a few minutes. The show was a failure and closed after eight months.

Berlin's long Broadway career was over, although Hollywood had not forgotten him. In 1964, a group of producers decided to make a film based on Irving Berlin songs. *Say It with Music* would be a lavish production, like the Music Box revues. The MGM movie studio paid Irving one million dollars for the rights to use his music. But after five years of planning, the project was canceled. MGM had decided that Irving Berlin's name would not sell.

For the next few decades, Irving Berlin lived a quiet and solitary life. With no more interest in working on Broadway or in the movies, he stopped writing songs. Many of his old friends passed away. His sisters and brothers had died, and he lost Ellin in 1988. For another year, he lived with his memories in his apartment in New York. In 1989 he died, at the age of 101.

Bibliography

Bergreen, Lawrence. *As Thousands Cheer*. New York: Viking Penguin, 1990.

Berlin, Irving. *The Songs of Irving Berlin*. 5 vols. Milwaukee, Wisconsin: Hal Leonard, 1991.

Blesh, Rudi. *They All Played Ragtime*. New York: Knopf, 1950.

Ewen, David. *The Story of Irving Berlin*. New York: Henry Holt & Company, 1950.

Freedland, Michael. *Irving Berlin*. New York: Stein & Day, 1974.

Salsini, Barbara. *Irving Berlin, Master Composer of 20th Century Songs*. Charlottesville, Virginia: SamHar Press, 1972.

Woollcott, Alexander. *The Story of Irving Berlin*. New York: Da Capo Press Music Reprint Series, 1983.